The Official Sassafras Scidat Logbook

Zoology Edition

PREPARED BY: _____

THE OFFICIAL SASSAFRAS SCIDAT LOGBOOK: ZOOLOGY EDITION

Third Edition, First Printing 2022
Copyright @ Elemental Science, Inc.
Email: support@elementalscience.com

ISBN # 978-1-935614-23-4

Printed In USA For World Wide Distribution

For more copies write to :
Elemental Science
PO Box 79
Niceville, FL 32588
support@elementalscience.com

COPYRIGHT POLICY

The Official Sassafras SCIDAT Logbook: Zoology Edition

Table of Contents

SCIDAT* LOGBOOK AT-A-GLANCE

> *Document your adventure with the Sassafras Twins!*

1. HABITAT INFORMATION SHEET

The purpose of this sheet is for you to record what you have learned about the habitats visited in *The Sassafras Science Adventures Volume 1: Zoology.*

2. AROUND THE WORLD SHEET

The purpose of this sheet is to give you an opportunity to work on your mapping skills.

3. ANIMAL RECORD SHEET

The purpose of this sheet is for you to record what you have learned about the animals that are introduced in *The Sassafras Science Adventures Volume 1: Zoology.*

4. PROJECT RECORD SHEET

The purpose of this sheet is for you to record the projects you have completed throughout the course of your study of zoology.

5. ZOOLOGY NOTES SHEET

The purpose of this sheet is for you to record any additional information you have learned during your study of zoology.

6. ZOOLOGY GLOSSARY

The purpose of the glossary is for you to create a glossary of vocabulary terms you have encountered throughout your reading of *The Sassafras Science Adventures Volume 1: Zoology.*

*SCIDAT stands for "**sci**entific **dat**a" and it comes from the app that the Sassafras Twins use on their journey.

SCIDAT Logbook
Zoology Notes: Observation

SCIDAT Logbook
Zoology Notes: Observation

_____

_____

_____

_____

_____

_____

_____

_____

_____

_____

_____

_____

_____

_____

_____

_____

_____

SCIDAT Logbook
Habitat Information Sheet

Habitat

Location & Local Expert

Average Rainfall

Average Temperature

Main Characteristics

Animals Found There

SCIDAT Logbook
Grasslands Around the World

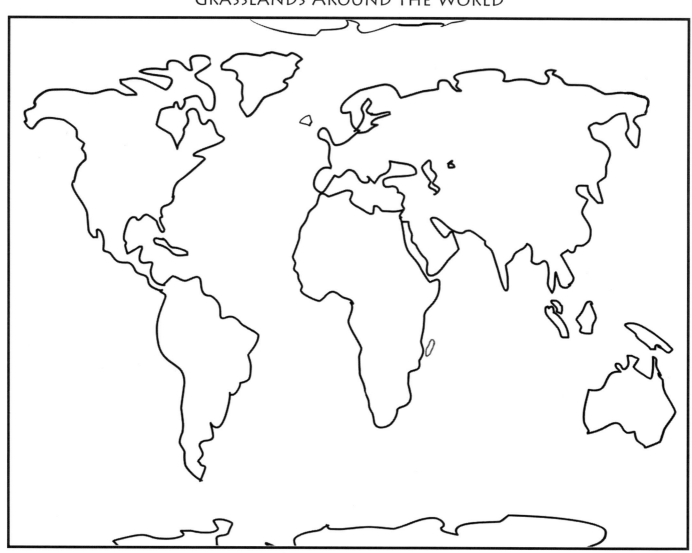

CONTINENTS FOUND ON...

SCIDAT Logbook
Animal Record Sheet

Animal Name

Classification

Food

Location Found

Information Learned

SCIDAT Logbook
ANIMAL RECORD SHEET

ANIMAL NAME

CLASSIFICATION

FOOD

LOCATION FOUND

INFORMATION LEARNED

SCIDAT Logbook
Animal Record Sheet

Animal Name

Classification

Food

Location Found

Information Learned

SCIDAT Logbook
Animal Record Sheet

Animal Name

Classification

Food

Location Found

Information Learned

SCIDAT Logbook
Zoology Notes: African Grasslands

_____

_____

_____

_____

_____

_____

_____

_____

_____

_____

_____

_____

_____

_____

_____

_____

_____

_____

SCIDAT Logbook
Zoology Notes: African Grasslands

_____
_____
_____
_____
_____
_____
_____
_____
_____
_____
_____
_____
_____

_____
_____
_____
_____

SCIDAT Logbook
Project Record Sheet

Glue Picture of
Project Here

Information Learned

SCIDAT Logbook
Project Record Sheet

GLUE PICTURE OF
PROJECT HERE

INFORMATION LEARNED

SCIDAT Logbook
Habitat Information Sheet

Habitat

Location & Local Expert

Average Rainfall

Average Temperature

Main Characteristics

Animals Found There

SCIDAT Logbook
Deserts Around the World

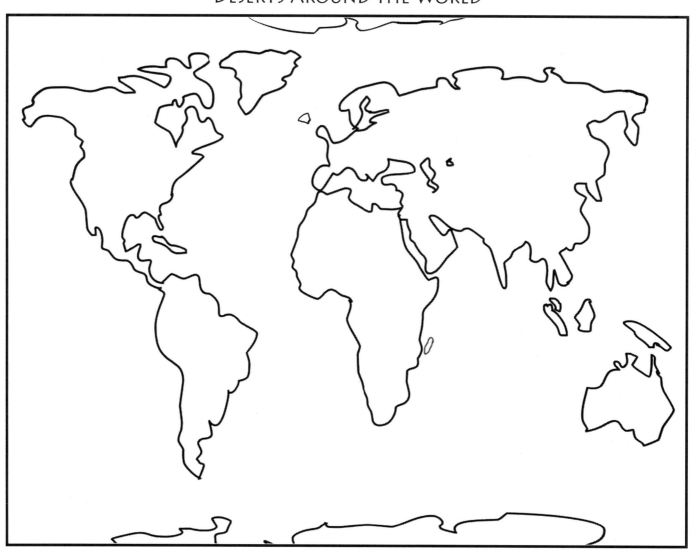

Continents found on...

SCIDAT Logbook
Animal Record Sheet

Animal Name

Classification

Food

Location Found

Information Learned

SCIDAT Logbook
Animal Record Sheet

Animal Name

Classification

Food

Location Found

Information Learned

SCIDAT Logbook
Animal Record Sheet

Animal Name

Classification

Food

Location Found

Information Learned

SCIDAT Logbook
Animal Record Sheet

Animal Name

Classification

Food

Location Found

Information Learned

SCIDAT Logbook
Zoology Notes: Egyptian Desert

_____

_____

_____

_____

_____

_____

_____

_____

_____

_____

_____

_____

                                    _____

                                    _____

                                    _____

                                    _____

SCIDAT Logbook
Zoology Notes: Egyptian Desert

_____

_____

_____

_____

_____

_____

_____

_____

_____

_____

_____

_____

                                    _____

                                    _____

                                    _____

                                    _____

SCIDAT Logbook
Project Record Sheet

Glue Picture of
Project Here

Information Learned

SCIDAT Logbook
Project Record Sheet

Glue Picture of
Project Here

Information Learned

SCIDAT Logbook
Habitat Information Sheet

Habitat

Location & Local Expert

Average Rainfall

Average Temperature

Main Characteristics

Animals Found There

SCIDAT Logbook
Domestic Farms Around the World

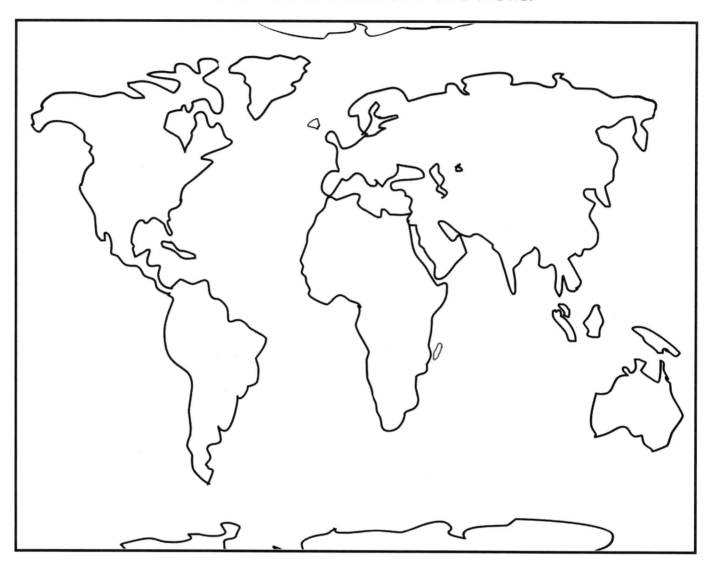

CONTINENTS FOUND ON...

SCIDAT Logbook
Animal Record Sheet

Animal Name

Classification

Food

Location Found

Information Learned

SCIDAT Logbook
Animal Record Sheet

Animal Name

Classification

Food

Location Found

Information Learned

SCIDAT Logbook
Animal Record Sheet

Animal Name

Classification

Food

Location Found

Information Learned

SCIDAT Logbook
Animal Record Sheet

Animal Name

Classification

Food

Location Found

Information Learned

SCIDAT Logbook
Zoology Notes: Canadian Farm

_____

_____

_____

_____

_____

_____

_____

_____

_____

_____

_____

_____

_____

_____

_____

_____

SCIDAT Logbook
Zoology Notes: Canadian Farm

_____

_____

_____

_____

_____

_____

_____

_____

_____

_____

_____

_____

_____

_____

_____

_____

_____

SCIDAT Logbook
Project Record Sheet

GLUE PICTURE OF
PROJECT HERE

Information Learned

SCIDAT Logbook
Project Record Sheet

Information Learned

SCIDAT Logbook
Habitat Information Sheet

Habitat

Location & Local Expert

Average Rainfall

Average Temperature

Main Characteristics

Animals Found There

SCIDAT Logbook
Rainforests Around the World

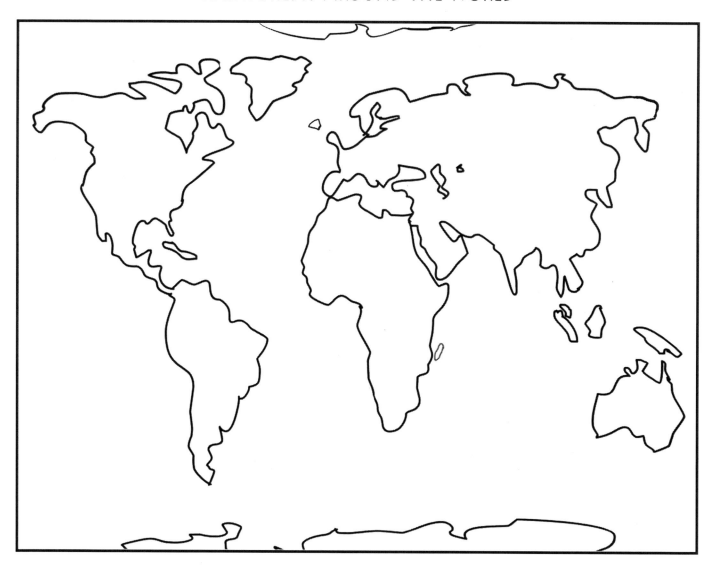

CONTINENTS FOUND ON...

SCIDAT Logbook
Animal Record Sheet

Animal Name

Classification

Food

Location Found

Information Learned

SCIDAT Logbook
Animal Record Sheet

Animal Name

Classification

Food

Location Found

Information Learned

SCIDAT Logbook
Animal Record Sheet

Animal Name

Classification

Food

Location Found

Information Learned

SCIDAT Logbook
Animal Record Sheet

Animal Name

Classification

Food

Location Found

Information Learned

SCIDAT Logbook
Zoology Notes: Rainforest

_____

_____

_____

_____

_____

_____

_____

_____

_____

_____

_____

_____

_____

SCIDAT Logbook
Zoology Notes: Rainforest

_____

_____

_____

_____

_____

_____

_____

_____

_____

_____

_____

_____

SCIDAT Logbook
Project Record Sheet

GLUE PICTURE OF
PROJECT HERE

INFORMATION LEARNED

SCIDAT Logbook
Project Record Sheet

GLUE PICTURE OF
PROJECT HERE

INFORMATION LEARNED

SCIDAT Logbook
Habitat Information Sheet

Habitat

Location & Local Expert

Average Rainfall

Average Temperature

Main Characteristics

Animals Found There

SCIDAT Logbook
Eucalyptus Forests Around the World

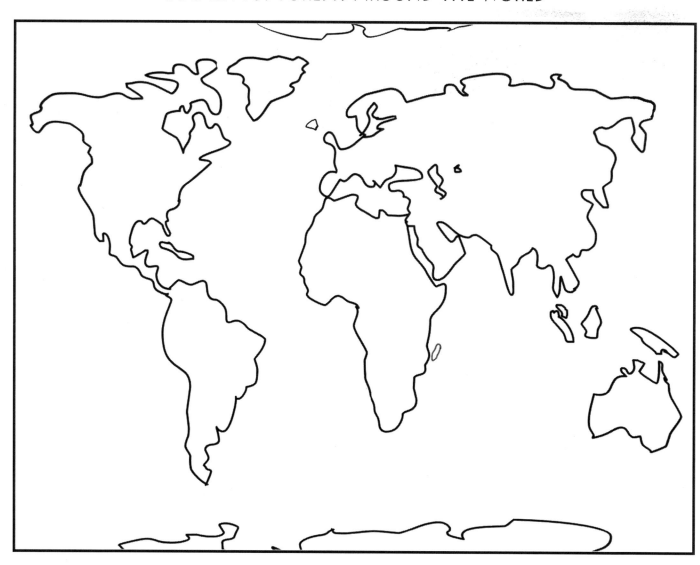

CONTINENTS FOUND ON...

SCIDAT Logbook
Animal Record Sheet

Animal Name

Classification

Food

Location Found

Information Learned

SCIDAT Logbook
Animal Record Sheet

Animal Name

Classification

Food

Location Found

Information Learned

SCIDAT Logbook
Animal Record Sheet

ANIMAL NAME

CLASSIFICATION

FOOD

LOCATION FOUND

INFORMATION LEARNED

SCIDAT Logbook
Animal Record Sheet

Animal Name

Classification

Food

Location Found

Information Learned

SCIDAT Logbook
Zoology Notes: Eucalyptus forest

_____

_____

_____

_____

_____

_____

_____

_____

_____

                          _____

                          _____

                          _____

SCIDAT Logbook
Zoology Notes: Eucalyptus forest

_____
_____
_____
_____
_____
_____
_____
_____
_____
_____

_____
_____

_____

SCIDAT Logbook
Project Record Sheet

GLUE PICTURE OF
PROJECT HERE

INFORMATION LEARNED

SCIDAT Logbook
Project Record Sheet

GLUE PICTURE OF
PROJECT HERE

Information Learned

SCIDAT Logbook
Habitat Information Sheet

Habitat

Location & Local Expert

Average Rainfall

Average Temperature

Main Characteristics

Animals Found There

SCIDAT Logbook
Bamboo Forests Around the World

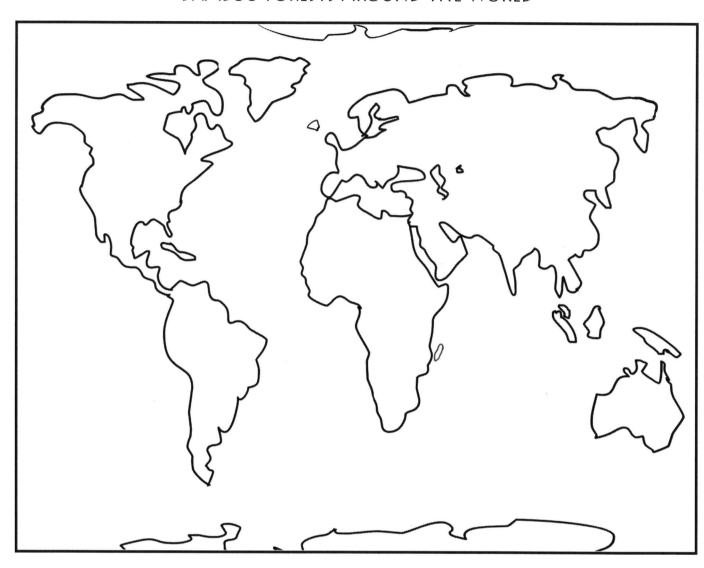

CONTINENTS FOUND ON...

SCIDAT Logbook
Animal Record Sheet

Animal Name

Classification

Food

Location Found

Information Learned

SCIDAT Logbook
Animal Record Sheet

Animal Name

Classification

Food

Location Found

Information Learned

SCIDAT Logbook
Animal Record Sheet

Animal Name

Classification

Food

Location Found

Information Learned

SCIDAT LOGBOOK
ANIMAL RECORD SHEET

ANIMAL NAME

CLASSIFICATION

FOOD

LOCATION FOUND

INFORMATION LEARNED

SCIDAT Logbook

Zoology Notes: Bamboo forest

SCIDAT Logbook
Zoology Notes: Bamboo forest

SCIDAT Logbook
Project Record Sheet

GLUE PICTURE OF
PROJECT HERE

INFORMATION LEARNED

SCIDAT Logbook
Project Record Sheet

Glue Picture of
Project Here

Information Learned

SCIDAT Logbook
Habitat Information Sheet

Habitat

Location & Local Expert

Average Rainfall

Average Temperature

Main Characteristics

Animals Found There

SCIDAT Logbook
Arctic Habitats Around the World

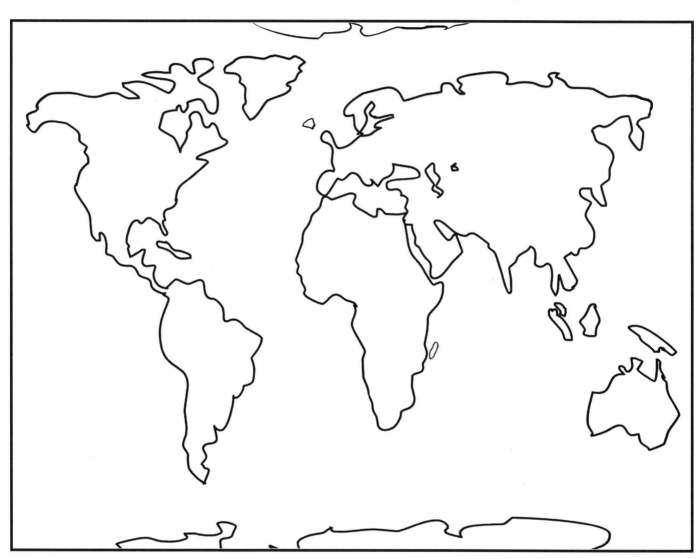

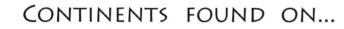

CONTINENTS FOUND ON...

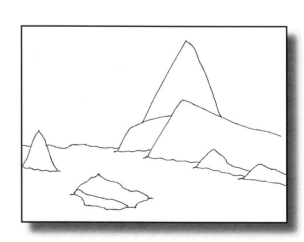

SCIDAT Logbook
Animal Record Sheet

Animal Name

Classification

Food

Location Found

Information Learned

SCIDAT LOGBOOK
ANIMAL RECORD SHEET

ANIMAL NAME

CLASSIFICATION

FOOD

LOCATION FOUND

INFORMATION LEARNED

SCIDAT Logbook
Animal Record Sheet

Animal Name

Classification

Food

Location Found

Information Learned

SCIDAT Logbook
Animal Record Sheet

Animal Name

Classification

Food

Location Found

Information Learned

SCIDAT Logbook
Zoology Notes: Arctic

_____

_____

_____

_____

_____

_____

_____

_____

_____

_____

_____

_____

_____

_____

SCIDAT Logbook
Zoology Notes: Arctic

SCIDAT Logbook
Project Record Sheet

GLUE PICTURE OF
PROJECT HERE

INFORMATION LEARNED

SCIDAT Logbook
Project Record Sheet

Glue Picture of
Project Here

Information Learned

SCIDAT Logbook
Habitat Information Sheet

Habitat

Location & Local Expert

Average Rainfall

Average Temperature

Main Characteristics

Animals Found There

SCIDAT Logbook
Oceans Around the World

SCIDAT Logbook
Animal Record Sheet

Animal Name

Classification

Food

Location Found

Information Learned

SCIDAT LOGBOOK
ANIMAL RECORD SHEET

ANIMAL NAME

CLASSIFICATION

FOOD

LOCATION FOUND

INFORMATION LEARNED

SCIDAT Logbook
Animal Record Sheet

Animal Name

Classification

Food

Location Found

Information Learned

SCIDAT Logbook
Animal Record Sheet

Animal Name

Classification

Food

Location Found

Information Learned

SCIDAT Logbook
Zoology Notes: Ocean

_____

_____

_____

_____

_____

_____

_____

_____

_____

_____

_____

_____

_____

SCIDAT Logbook
Zoology Notes: Ocean

_____

_____

_____

_____

_____

_____

_____

_____

_____

_____

_____

_____

_____

SCIDAT Logbook
Project Record Sheet

GLUE PICTURE OF
PROJECT HERE

INFORMATION LEARNED

SCIDAT Logbook
Project Record Sheet

Glue Picture of
Project Here

Information Learned

SCIDAT Logbook
Zoology Notes: Bonus Data

_____

_____

_____

_____

_____

_____

_____

_____

_____

_____

BONUS DATA

METHODS OF DEFENSE

1.) Playing dead
   The prey acts as if they are already dead, which can shut off the hunting behavior in a predator.

2.) Making an escape
   The prey makes a sudden dash for safety. This method relies on the fact that the prey is fast and has sharp senses.

3.) Spines or scales
   The prey is covered with spines or scales which make it difficult for the predator to eat it.

_____

_____

_____

_____

_____

_____

_____

_____

_____

_____

SCIDAT Logbook

_____

_____

_____

_____

_____

_____

_____

_____

_____

_____

_____

_____

_____

_____

_____

_____

_____

BONUS DATA

for the predator to eat it.

4.) Camouflage
   The prey disguises itself as something else so that the predator cannot find it.

5.) Mimicry
   The prey mimics another more dangerous animal so that the predator will leave it alone.

6.) Chemical weapons
   The prey emits a poisonous or foul-smelling chemical to keep predators from eating it.

DIET
Carnivores are meat-eaters

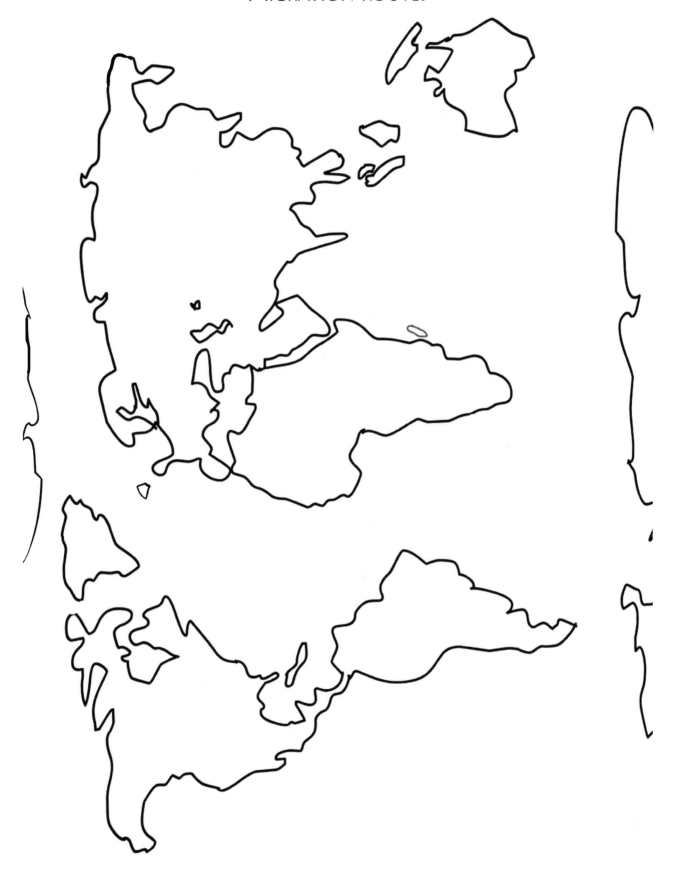

Zoology Glossary

Zoology Vocabulary

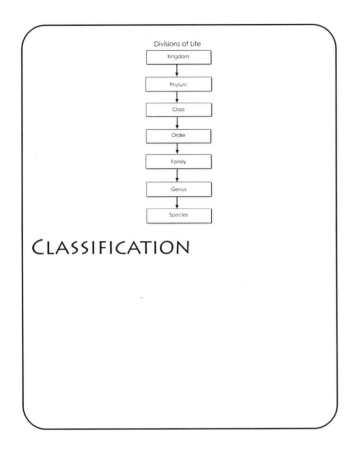

Classification

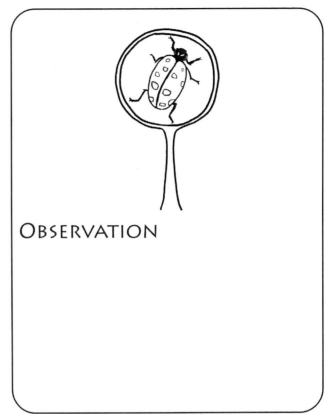

Observation

Food Chain

Grasslands

Zoology Vocabulary

Mammal

Herbivore

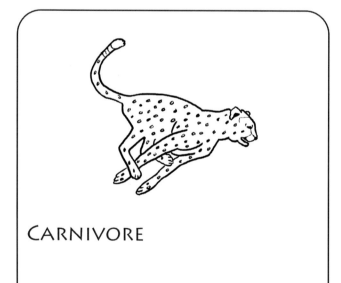

Carnivore

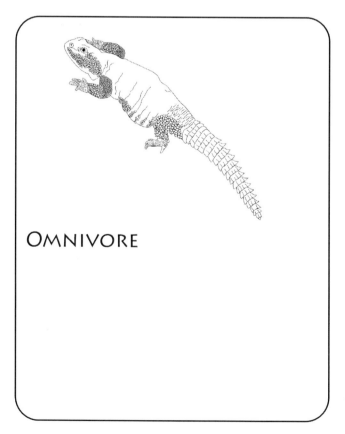

Omnivore

Zoology Vocabulary

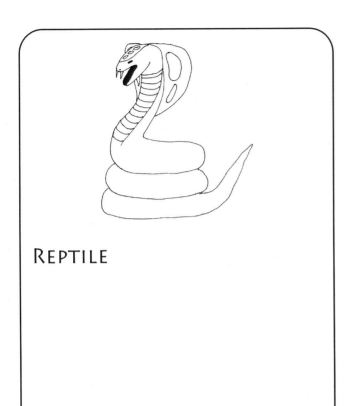

Reptile

Desert

Domesticated Animal

Arthropod

Zoology Vocabulary

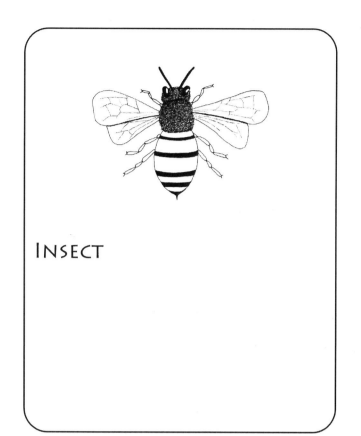

Insect

Rainforest

Amphibian

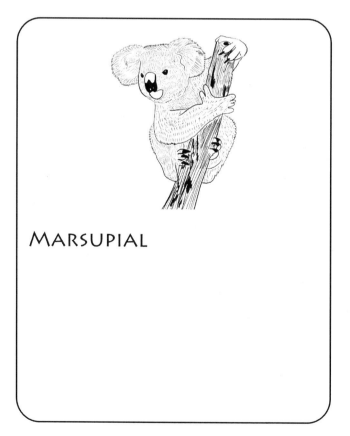

Marsupial

Zoology Vocabulary

BIRD

FOREST

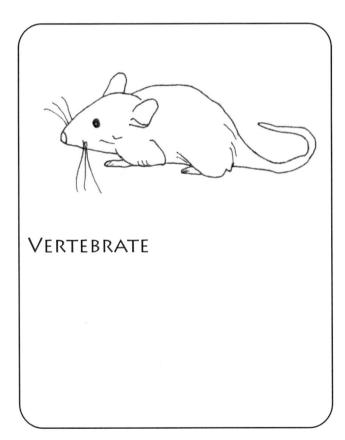

VERTEBRATE

ARCTIC

Zoology Vocabulary

Hibernation

Ocean

Fish

Invertebrate

Zoology Vocabulary

Migration

Made in United States
North Haven, CT
16 June 2023